"Thou Shalt Love The Lord Thy God With All Thy Heart, And With All Thy Soul, And With All Thy Mind."

–Matthew 22:37

"What You Love The Most Will Reward You."

-MIKE MURDOCK

2

"Honour Thy Father And Thy Mother: And, Thou Shalt Love Thy Neighbour As Thyself."

–Matthew 19:19

"The King Within You Will Awaken The King In Another."
-MIKE MURDOCK

3

"For God So Loved The World, That He Gave His Only Begotten Son, That Whosoever Believeth In Him Should Not Perish, But Have Everlasting Life. "

-John 3:16

"The Proof Of Love Is The Desire To Give."
-MIKE MURDOCK

4

"By This Shall All Men Know That Ye Are My Disciples, If Ye Have Love One To Another."

–John 13:35

"The Proof Of Love Is The Passion To Pleasure."
-MIKE MURDOCK

5

"Greater Love Hath No Man Than This, That A Man Lay Down His Life For His Friends."

–John 15:13

"Champions Walk Away From Something They Desire To Protect Something Else They Love."
-MIKE MURDOCK

"Love Worketh No Ill To His Neighbour: Therefore Love Is The Fulfilling Of The Law."

–Romans 13:10

"Ultimately Love Is The Only Law."
-MIKE MURDOCK

7

"Though I Speak With The Tongues Of Men And Of Angels, And Have Not Charity, I Am Become As Sounding Brass, Or A Tinkling Cymbal."

-1 Corinthians 13:1

"Skillful Words Are Not The Proof Of Love."
-MIKE MURDOCK

8

"And To Know The Love Of Christ, Which Passeth Knowledge, That Ye Might Be Filled With All The Fulness Of God."

–Ephesians 3:19

*"The Greater Your Love For God...
The Greater Your Love For People."*
-MIKE MURDOCK

9

"Beloved, Let Us Love One Another: For Love Is Of God; And Every One That Loveth Is Born Of God, And Knoweth God."

–1 John 4:7

"The Presence Of God Will Birth Your Ability To Love."

-MIKE MURDOCK

10

"Herein Is Love, Not That We Loved God, But That He Loved Us, And Sent His Son To Be The Propitiation For Our Sins."

–1 John 4:10

"The Proof Of Love Is The Willingness To Reach."
-MIKE MURDOCK

11

"Beloved, If God So Loved Us, We Ought Also To Love One Another."

-1 John 4:11

"Your Willingness To Receive Love Determines
Your Ability To Sow Love."

-MIKE MURDOCK

12

"If We Love One Another, God Dwelleth In Us, And His Love Is Perfected In Us."

-1 John 4:12

"The Proof Of God Is The Presence Of Love."
-MIKE MURDOCK

13

"And We Have Known And Believed The Love That God Hath To Us. God Is Love; And He That Dwelleth In Love Dwelleth In God, And God In Him."

-1 John 4:16

"Disconnecting From God Dissolves Your Capability To Love."
-MIKE MURDOCK

14

"There Is No Fear In Love; But Perfect Love Casteth Out Fear: Because Fear Hath Torment. He That Feareth Is Not Made Perfect In Love."

-1 John 4:18

"The Proof Of Love Is The Absence Of Fear."
-MIKE MURDOCK

15

"We Love Him, Because He First Loved Us."

–1 John 4:19

"You Can Only Give Away Something You Have Received."
-MIKE MURDOCK

16

"For Whom The Lord Loveth He Chasteneth, And Scourgeth Every Son Whom He Receiveth."

–Hebrews 12:6

*"The Proof Of Love
Is The Willingness To Correct."*
-MIKE MURDOCK

17

"And Now Abideth Faith, Hope, Charity, These Three; But The Greatest Of These Is Charity."

-1 Corinthians 13:13

"The Products Of Love Are Faith And Hope."
-MIKE MURDOCK

18

"If Ye Love Me,
Keep My
Commandments."

–John 14:15

"The Proof Of Love
Is The Willingness To Obey."
-MIKE MURDOCK

19

"Hereby Perceive We The Love Of God, Because He Laid Down His Life For Us: And We Ought To Lay Down Our Lives For The Brethren."

–1 John 3:16

"The Proof Of Love
Is The Desire To Protect."
-MIKE MURDOCK

20

"But Whoso Hath This World's Good, And Seeth His Brother Have Need, And Shutteth Up His Bowels Of Compassion From Him, How Dwelleth The Love Of God In Him?"

−1 John 3:17

"What You Truly Love You Cannot Ignore."

−MIKE MURDOCK

21

"My Little Children, Let Us Not Love In Word, Neither In Tongue; But In Deed And In Truth."

–1 John 3:18

"What You Do Is What You Are."
-MIKE MURDOCK

22

"For I Am Persuaded, That Neither Death, Nor Life, Nor Angels, Nor Principalities, Nor Powers, Nor Things Present, Nor Things To Come, Nor Height, Nor Depth, Nor Any Other Creature, Shall Be Able To Separate Us From The Love Of God, Which Is In Christ Jesus Our Lord."

-Romans 8:38,39

"Ultimately Everything Succumbs To The Power Of Love."
                              -MIKE MURDOCK

23

"But I Say Unto You, Love Your Enemies, Bless Them That Curse You, Do Good To Them That Hate You, And Pray For Them Which Despitefully Use You, And Persecute You."

–Matthew 5:44

"If You Want Something You Have Never Had—You Have To Do Something You Have Never Done."

-MIKE MURDOCK

24

"For If Ye Love Them Which Love You, What Thank Have Ye? For Sinners Also Love Those That Love Them."

–Luke 6:32

"Love Never Needs A Reason."
-MIKE MURDOCK

25

"Husbands, Love Your Wives, Even As Christ Also Loved The Church, And Gave Himself For It."

–Ephesians 5:25

"Your Reaction To Your Mate Reveals Your Opinion Of God."
-MIKE MURDOCK

26

"Charity Suffereth Long, And Is Kind; Charity Envieth Not; Charity Vaunteth Not Itself, Is Not Puffed Up, Beareth All Things, Believeth All Things, Hopeth All Things, Endureth All Things."

–1 Corinthians 13:4,7

"The Proof Of Love Is The Ability To Endure."
-MIKE MURDOCK

27

"Yea, I Have Loved Thee With An Everlasting Love: Therefore With Lovingkindness Have I Drawn Thee."

-Jeremiah 31:3

"Love Draws...Not Dominates."
-MIKE MURDOCK

28

"...Because The Love Of God Is Shed Abroad In Our Hearts By The Holy Ghost Which Is Given Unto Us." —Romans 5:5

"Holy Love Is The Product Of The Holy Spirit."
-MIKE MURDOCK

29

"A Friend Loveth At All Times, And A Brother Is Born For Adversity." —Proverbs 17:17

"The Proof Of Love Is The Inability To Betray."
-MIKE MURDOCK

30

"Hatred Stirreth Up Strifes: But Love Covereth All Sins."

–Proverbs 10:12

"What Hate Reveals—
Love Conceals."

-MIKE MURDOCK

31

"But God Commendeth His Love Toward Us, In That, While We Were Yet Sinners, Christ Died For Us."
-Romans 5:8

"Love Is The Seed For Change."
-MIKE MURDOCK

DECISION

Will You Accept Jesus As Your Personal Savior Today?

The Bible says, "That if thou shalt confess with thy mouth the Lord Jesus, and shalt believe in thine heart that God hath raised Him from the dead, thou shalt be saved" (Romans 10:9).

Pray this prayer from your heart today! *"Dear Jesus, I believe that You died for me and rose again on the third day. I confess I am a sinner...I need Your love and forgiveness...Come into my heart. Forgive my sins. I receive Your eternal life. Confirm Your love by giving me peace, joy and supernatural love for others. Amen."*

☐ Yes, Mike! I made a decision to accept Christ as my personal Savior today. Please send me my free gift of your book *"31 Keys to a New Beginning"* to help me with my new life in Christ. *(B-48)*

NAME _____

ADDRESS _____

CITY _____ STATE _____ ZIP _____

PHONE ( ) _____ EMAIL _____

Mail To: **The Wisdom Center**   *(B-173)*
P.O. Box 99 · Denton, TX 76202
1-888-WISDOM-1 (1-888-947-3661)
Website: www.thewisdomcenter.tv

Unless otherwise indicated, all Scripture quotations are taken from the King James Version of the Bible.
Memory Bible On Love · ISBN 1-56394-265-8/B-173
Copyright © 2003 by **MIKE MURDOCK**
All publishing rights belong exclusively to Wisdom International
Published by The Wisdom Center · P.O. Box 99 · Denton, Texas 76202
1-888-WISDOM-1 (1-888-947-3661) · Website: www.thewisdomcenter.tv
Printed in the United States of America. All rights reserved under International Copyright Law. Contents and/or cover may not be reproduced in whole or in part in any form without the expressed written consent of the publisher.   03030

THE WISDOM CENTER

1-888-WISDOM-1 (1-888-947-3661)

Mon.-Fri.
8 AM-5 PM CST

visit us at:
www.thewisdomcenter.cc

PRODUCT NUMBER	PRODUCT DESCRIPTION	QTY	PRICE	TOTAL
				1
				2
				3
				4
				5
				6

SubTotal	$	7
Canada ADD 20%	$	8
S/H Add 10%	$	9
TOTAL	$	10
My Seed Offering	$	11

Bookstore Discounts
(assorted titles!)

QTY.	DISCOUNT
1-9	Retail
10-499	40%
500-1999	50%
2000-4999	60%
5000 & Up	Contact Office

Name

Address

City _____ State _____ Zip

Phone _____ Email

Method of Payment
☐ Cash ☐ Check ☐ Visa ☐ MC ☐ Amex ☐ Discover

Card#

Birthday ___ MO ___ DAY   Expiration Date

Total Enclosed $ _____ Signature

(Sorry No C.O.D.'s)

Your Seed Faith Offering is used to support the MIKE MURDOCK Evangelistic Association, The Wisdom Center, and all its programs. Applicable law requires that we have the discretion to allocate donations in order to carry out our charitable purpose. In the event MMEA receives more funds for the project than needed, excess will be used for another worthy outreach.

B-173

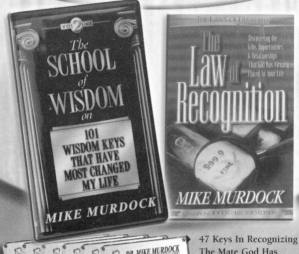

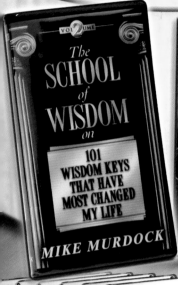
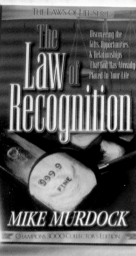

Financial Success.

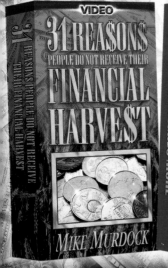

8 Scriptural Reasons You Should Pursue Financial Prosperity

The Secret Prayer Key You Need When Making A Financial Request To God

The Weapon Of Expectation And The 5 Miracles It Unlocks

How To Discern Those Who Qualify To Receive Your Financial Assistance

How To Predict The Miracle Moment God Will Schedule Your Financial Breakthrough

Habits Of Uncommon Achievers

The Greatest Success Law I Ever Discovered

▸ How To Discern Your Place Of Assignment, The Only Place Financial Provision Is Guaranteed

▸ 3 Secret Keys In Solving Problems For Others

The Wisdom Center
Video Pak
AMVIDEO **$30**
Buy 1-Get 1 Free
(A $60 Value!)
Wisdom Is The Principal Thing

Add 10% For S/H

Songs From The Secret Place.

The Music Ministry of MIKE MURDOCK

SONGS FROM THE SECRET PLACE
Love Songs To The Holy Spirit
Birthed In The Secret Place

THE HOLY SPIRIT HANDBOOK
What You Need To Know About Your
Daily Companion, The Holy Spirit
Volume 1
MIKE MURDOCK

Songs...

1. A Holy Place
2. Anything You Want
3. Everything Comes From You
4. Fill This Place With Your Presence
5. First Thing Every Morning
6. Holy Spirit, I Want To Hear You
7. Holy Spirit, Move Again
8. Holy Spirit, You Are Enough
9. I Don't Know What I Would Do Without You
10. I Let Go (Of Anything That Stops Me)
11. I'll Just Fall On You
12. I Love You, Holy Spirit
13. I'm Building My Life Around You
14. I'm Giving Myself To You
15. I'm In Love! I'm In Love!
16. I Need Water (Holy Spirit, You're My Well)
17. In The Secret Place
18. In Your Presence, I'm Always Changed
19. In Your Presence
20. I've Got To Live In Your Presence
21. I Want To Hear Your Voice
22. I Will Do Things Your Way
23. Just One Day At A Time
24. Meet Me In The Secret Place
25. More Than Ever Before
26. Nobody Else Does What You Do
27. No Walls!
28. Nothing Else Matters Anymore (Since I've Been In The Presence Of You Lord)
29. Nowhere Else
30. Once Again You've Answered
31. Only A Fool Would Try (To Live Without You)
32. Take Me Now
33. Teach Me How To Please You
34. There's No Place I'd Rather Be
35. Thy Word Is All That Matters
36. When I Get In Your Presence
37. You're The Best Thing (That's Ever Happened To Me)
38. You Are Wonderful
39. You've Done It Once
40. You Keep Changing Me
41. You Satisfy

Add 10% For S/H

The Uncommon Woman

- Master Keys In Understanding The Man In Your Life
- The One Thing Every Man Attempts To Move Away From
- The Dominant Difference Between A Wrong Woman And A Right Woman
- What Causes Men To Withdraw

MIKE MURDOCK

THE WISDOM FOR WOMEN SERIES

THIRTY-ONE SECRETS of an UNFORGETTABLE WOMAN

Master Secrets from the Life of Ruth

THE WISDOM CENTER
MIKE MURDOCK • P.O. Box 99 • Denton, Texas

31 Secrets of an Unforgettable Woman

THE **PROVERBS 31** Woman

MIKE MURDOCK
MENTORSHIP PROGRAM OF WISDOM

The Wisdom Center
6 Tapes | $30
PAK-009
Wisdom Is The Principal Thing

Free Book Enclosed!
Wisdom Is The Principal Thing

UNCOMMON WISDOM FOR AN UNCOMMON MINISTRY

FOR *Ministers* ONLY

THE UNCOMMON MINISTER — Power Principles For Hitting Your Target For Success in Ministry — MIKE MURDOCK — 1

THE UNCOMMON MINISTER — Wisdom Keys For A Ministry Of Excellence And Greatness — MIKE MURDOCK — 2

THE UNCOMMON MINISTER — Wisdom Principles For Achieving Greatness in Your Ministry — 3

THE UNCOMMON MINISTER — Principles On The Path To A Victorious Ministry — 4

THE UNCOMMON MINISTER — Sign Posts On The Road To Excellence in Ministry — MIKE MURDOCK — 5

THE UNCOMMON MINISTER — Powerful Steps To A More Powerful Ministry — MIKE MURDOCK — 6

THE UNCOMMON MINISTER — Steps To Achieving Your Goals in Your Ministry — MIKE MURDOCK — 7

Volume 1	B-10
Volume 2	B-10
Volume 3	B-10
Volume 4	B-1
Volume 5	B-1
Volume 6	B-1
Volume 7	B-1

When God wants to touch a nation, He raises up a preacher. It is Uncommon Men and Women of God who have driven back the darkness and shielded the unlearned and rebellious from devastation by satanic forces. They offer the breath of life to a dead world. They open Golden Doors to Change. They unleash Forces of Truth in an age of deception.

An Uncommon Minister is prepared through seasons of pain, encounters with God, and mentors. Having sat at the feet of Uncommon Mentors his entire life, Dr. Mike Murdock shares practical but personal keys to increase the excellence and productivity of your ministry. Each volume of "The Uncommon Minister" is handy, convenient and easy to read. Your load will be lighter, your journey happier, and your effectiveness increased in "doing the will of the Father.

Add 10% For S/H

F

THE WISDOM CENTER
P.O. Box 99, Denton, Texas 76202

1-888-WISDOM1
(1-888-947-3661)

Website:
WWW.THEWISDOMCENTER.TV

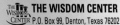